PRAVEEN KOTTEPAKA

Silent Sufferings of Men

Dealing with a Difficult Marriage

TANISHQ
PAGE PORT PUBLICATIONS

Contents

Preface

The silent battles they fight behind closed doors are often overlooked in a world that usually paints men as the unwavering pillars of strength. As society progresses, allowing women to express their struggles, the emotional and psychological toll that many men bear in their relationships remains hidden. The book Silent Sufferings of Men seeks to break the silence.

This is more than just another self-help guide. It is a deeply personal exploration of a topic that many men around the world face but rarely discuss: how to navigate the complex and often toxic dynamics of a relationship with a difficult spouse. For many men, marriage or partnership turns into a battleground of emotional manipulation, false accusations, and never-ending expectations. However, societal norms and long-held expectations frequently prevent men from speaking up or seeking assistance. Many men suffer silently because they are afraid of being labeled "weak" or "unmanly."

In this book, I hope to disprove these misconceptions. Drawing on real-life stories, societal trends, and psychological insights, I reveal the untold truth about what many men face daily: emotional abuse, constant belittling, and toxic manipulation. This is a story about survival and empowerment, not blame. It is a guide that will help men find their voice, regain their strength, and reclaim control of their lives.

Moreover, this book offers practical strategies tested and proven to help men in complex relationships. Whether you're feeling lost, angry, or confused, the following chapters will provide clarity, strength, and actionable steps. From understanding the psychology behind your spouse's behavior to learning to set healthy boundaries, this book will provide the tools to protect your emotional well-being and rebuild your confidence.

It's time for men to have a voice. It's time to stop suffering in silence.

So, to every man reading this who has ever felt invisible, unheard, or unappreciated, this book is for you. It is a call to action to take charge of your situation and realize that you are not alone on this journey. Together, we'll discover how to deal with a difficult wife and reclaim your peace of mind.

This is your moment to break free. Let the journey begin

Acknowledgments

I am deeply grateful to everyone who supported me in bringing *Silent Sufferings of Men.*I want to express my heartfelt gratitude to my dear friend **Balbeer Sing Thakur**, whose brilliantly designed cartoons have added a unique and meaningful touch to this book. His creativity has brought the themes and ideas to life, making them more engaging and relatable for readers.

I thank my family, friends, and all who encouraged me throughout this journey for your unwavering support.

Finally, I dedicate this book to all the silent sufferers whose stories inspired me. These pages serve as a source of comfort and empowerment for men navigating challenging relationships.

With gratitude,

Praveen Kottepaka.

,

Introduction: The Silent Crisis

The Silent Struggles of Men in a Gender-Based Society

Since ancient times, societal norms and cultural narratives have portrayed women as embodying vulnerability and delicacy. They have been cherished, protected, and treated like glass and flowers, representing fragility and beauty. This seemingly noble perspective has resulted in a profoundly ingrained illusion that women are inherently more vulnerable and require constant protection. For centuries, this narrative has influenced laws, social norms, and public perceptions.

Almost every country in the world has extensive legal frameworks in place to protect women from various types of abuse and harassment. These laws are critical and have significantly impacted advancing gender equality and protecting women's rights. However, in its efforts to protect and empower women, society has frequently ignored the plight of men who suffer in silence.

Many men today find themselves in a paradoxical situation. While societal norms continue to prioritize women's safety, men who are subjected to emotional, psychological, or even physical abuse are frequently left without a voice or support system. The legal structures designed to protect women can sometimes be abused, and there have been numerous cases where women have used these systems to harass or manipulate men and their family members.

John's story is a telling example. John, a dedicated and loving husband, found himself at the receiving end of relentless verbal and emotional abuse from his wife, Lisa. Despite his best efforts to maintain peace and harmony at home, Lisa's manipulative behavior escalated. She threatened to use the legal system against him, knowing that the laws were in her favor. John's cries for help went unheard, as friends and family dismissed his experiences, unable to believe that a man could be a victim in his marriage.

John's experience is not an isolated incident. According to studies and surveys conducted around the world, a significant number of men face various forms of abuse and harassment in their relationships. However, these issues are rarely discussed in public, and men frequently feel ashamed to seek help. The societal expectation of men to be stoic, strong, and emotionally resilient exacerbates the problem, leaving many men silent. However, when men muster the courage to seek help, it is a powerful demonstration of their strength and resilience, inspiring hope for a better future.

One of the most significant challenges is the absence of legal protection for men. Many countries' domestic violence laws are heavily skewed toward protecting women, often overlooking the fact that men can also be victims. This legal imbalance not only perpetuates men's suffering but also fosters an environment in which their voices are routinely silenced.

Furthermore, there is a severe lack of societal support for men. Men are frequently discouraged from speaking up about their struggles for fear of ridicule or disbelief. Even in the male community, there is a notable lack of empathy and understanding. Men are taught to internalize their pain, which can have severe psychological consequences such as depression, anxiety, and, in extreme cases, suicidal ideation.

Addressing this issue necessitates a paradigm shift in societal attitudes and legal frameworks. It is critical to recognize that vulnerability and suffering are gender-neutral and that men, too, deserve protection and support. This book seeks to shed light on these unseen tragedies and advocate for a more balanced approach to domestic issues.

Understanding men's historical context and realities can help to create a more inclusive and supportive environment. It is time to dispel the myth that only women are vulnerable and acknowledge that men, too, can be victims. Only then can we hope to create a society in which all people, regardless of gender, have the right to live free of abuse and harassment? Your understanding and support are critical to creating a more equitable society, and they will enlighten us and foster empathy.

As you read this book, please consider these issues and how we can all work together to make our society more equitable and compassionate. The strategies and insights presented in the following chapters aim to empower men to take control of their lives and seek help without fear or shame.

Chapter 1: The Price of Silence: Alejandro's Lost Battle

In the quiet Spanish suburbs of an ordinary town lived a man named Alejandro, whose life seemed nothing short of perfect. Alejandro had always been remarkable, excelling in every endeavor he undertook. As a child, he was a brilliant student who topped every class, earning the admiration of his teachers and peers alike. His prowess matched his intelligence in sports, where he consistently led his school and college teams to victory. Alejandro wasn't just the academic star; he was the golden boy who seemed to have it all—good looks, charm, and the adoration of many girls who saw him as the hero of their dreams.

Alejandro's reputation went beyond the school grounds. Within his family, he was admired for his accomplishments, kindness, and generosity. He was always there to support his relatives, both financially and morally, serving as the pillar that held everyone together. His success carried over into adulthood when he rose to the top of a prestigious organization. Alejandro was a devoted husband, showering his wife with love, care, and attention. Alejandro represented the pinnacle of success to the outside world—a man with everything anyone could want.

A storm was brewing beneath this perfect facade, though. Alejandro's seemingly ideal life started to unravel when he noticed changes in his wife's behavior. The woman who had once been his closest confidante distanced herself emotionally. Alejandro became concerned when he noticed her growing closer to a coworker. Initially, he attempted to dismiss his suspicions, believing they were unfounded. But as time passed, the signs became more difficult to ignore. He confronted his wife for reassurance, but his concerns were met with denial and accusations. Instead of addressing the issue, she accused Alejandro of being paranoid and possessive.

The more Alejandro attempted to solve the problem, the more isolated he became. His wife's refusal to acknowledge his feelings, combined with her continued closeness to her colleague, sent Alejandro into a deep depression. The man who had once been the brightest star in his family and community was now a mere shadow of himself. His work began to suffer, and he distanced himself from those who had always regarded him as an inspiration. The final blow came when Alejandro discovered irrefutable evidence of his wife's infidelity. The woman he had loved and trusted had betrayed him, shattering his entire world.

In his despair, Alejandro believed there was no way out. The emotional and psychological pain became unbearable. Despite all of his life's success and admiration, Alejandro could not overcome the heartbreak and betrayal that consumed him. Alejandro, feeling ultimately defeated and alone, made the tragic decision to commit suicide, believing that it was the only way out of the agony he was experiencing.

Alejandro's story is a heartbreaking reminder that even those who appear to have everything can be undone by emotional and psychological turmoil. His life, once full of promise and potential, was shattered by the toxic dynamics of his marriage.

This marriage transitioned from a source of love and support to one of pain and despair. To add to the tragedy, Alejandro's wife quickly resumed her life. She remarried and began a new life, seemingly unconcerned about the devastation left behind.

But Alejandro's family's pain was far from over. His mother, sister, and close friends were devastated by his loss. Once a proud and vibrant woman, his mother had become a shadow of herself. She carried the unbearable grief of losing her beloved son and was left with a life that felt empty and meaningless. Every day was a living nightmare for her, and her pain served as a constant reminder of Alejandro's silent suffering. His sister and close friends were left to deal with grief and guilt, wondering if they could have done anything to save him.

This book, *Silent Sufferings of Men*, honors the memory of men like Alejandro, who suffer in silence and believe they have no one to turn to. Alejandro's tragic death emphasizes the importance of recognizing the signs of emotional and psychological abuse, understanding its effects on men, and taking proactive steps to address it. This book seeks to break the silence surrounding male suffering in marriage and to equip men with the tools they need to protect their mental and emotional well-being. Let Alejandro's story serve as both a cautionary tale and a call to action for all men: you are not alone, and there is always hope, even in the darkest times.

Chapter 2: Overview of the Silent Struggles Faced by Men in Difficult Marriages

Imagine waking up daily in a home that used to feel like a sanctuary but is now more like a battlefield. You carry the weight of unspoken pain while navigating an emotional minefield.

The person who was once your closest ally has become a constant source of conflict, and you remain silent. This is the reality for many men in troubled marriages.

Men in these situations frequently go through their struggles quietly, concealing their pain behind a facade of strength. Society has conditioned them to believe that vulnerability is a sign of weakness. They are instructed to be the rock, the unwavering support, and the silent protector. But beneath this stoic exterior is a heart that aches, a spirit worn down by their constant challenges.

Emotional Manipulation:

Consider the following scenario: every conversation feels like a mental chess game. Your spouse twists your words, casts doubt on your memories, and makes you question your sanity. This is the pernicious nature of emotional manipulation and gas lighting. Each day becomes a battle to maintain your reality and remember that your emotions and experiences are valid.

Excessive Control:

Consider the constant monitoring and restrictions, which make you feel more like a prisoner than a partner. Your decisions are scrutinized, and your autonomy is stifled. You feel trapped, unable to make even minor decisions without being criticized or punished. The house that was supposed to be your refuge now feels like a cage.

Constant Criticism:

Imagine the emotional toll of constant criticism. Whatever you do, it's never enough—the constant barrage of negative comments undermines your self-esteem. You begin to internalize the belief that you are inadequate and unworthy of love and respect. A steady state of self-doubt replaces the joy and confidence you once felt.

Emotional Neglect:

Imagine the loneliness of living with someone emotionally unavailable. Your attempts to communicate are met with indifference or dismissal. You feel invisible, and your emotional needs are ignored. The sense of isolation is profound, as the person you should be closest to seems far away.

Financial Control:

Imagine the frustration and helplessness that comes with financial control. You have limited access to money, and your spending is being monitored. You are made to feel incapable and dependent. The ability to choose your life is taken away, leaving you powerless.

The Unseen burden:

These silent struggles are not limited to a problematic spouse's overt actions. They represent the cumulative weight of years of emotional and psychological suffering. The toll it takes on your mental health, the way it erodes your sense of self, and the constant effort to move forward in the face of inner turmoil.

The Strength to Endure:

Despite these challenges, you persevere. You put on a brave face, go to work, care for your family, and perform your duties. You hope that things improve and that the person you fell in love with returns. But the silent suffering continues every day, and the burden becomes heavier.

A Call for Compassion and Understanding:

This book is dedicated to you and every man who has ever felt alone in his struggle. It encourages compassion and understanding, reminding you that your pain and struggles are valid. You are not alone and should be heard, supported, and understood.

As you read through the pages of this book, remember that your silent suffering does not have to determine your future. There is hope, strategies, and a way to heal and empower. We can break the silence and start the journey to a healthier, happier life.

Turn the page and let us walk this journey together, acknowledging our silent struggles and finding the strength to overcome them.

Chapter 3: Global Data on Domestic Violence Against Men

Domestic violence is frequently viewed through a narrow lens, with an emphasis on female victims. However, the purpose of this chapter is to shed light on an often-overlooked reality: men, too, are victims of domestic abuse, and the data to back this up is staggering. Across the globe, millions of men are silently subjected to physical, emotional, psychological, and even sexual violence from intimate partners. This issue is not limited to a specific region, culture, or society. It extends across borders, from the United States and the United Kingdom to Australia, Canada, India, and beyond.

Intimate Partner Violence (IPV) is defined as any behavior within an intimate relationship that results in physical, psychological, or sexual harm to those involved. IPV is a significant public health concern that affects people of all genders, ages, and socioeconomic backgrounds. It is usually characterized by a power imbalance in which one partner seeks control over the other. Here is a breakdown of what it entails.

Forms of IPV

Physical violence includes hitting, slapping, punching, kicking, or any other physical force.

Psychological or emotional abuse involves constant criticism, manipulation, threats, isolation, and coercive control that harms the victim's mental health.

Sexual violence refers to any non-consensual sexual activity, such as rape, unwanted contact, or coercing a partner into sexual activities.

Economic abuse involves controlling or restricting access to financial resources, leaving the victim financially dependent.

Who is Affected

IPV can affect anyone, regardless of gender, but women have historically been the most commonly identified victims. However, recent research has shown that men are also affected by IPV, which is frequently under reported due to social stigma and gender norms.

Victims may experience injuries, chronic pain, or other physical health concerns. Victims of IPV frequently experience mental health issues such as anxiety, depression, and PTSD. IPV can isolate victims from family and friends, reducing support networks and leading to feelings of helplessness.

Intimate partner violence (IPV) is a pervasive problem affecting millions worldwide regardless of race, age, and socioeconomic status. IPV includes a progressive pattern of abusive behavior that can be physical, emotional, psychological, and sexual.

In the U.S., police receive more than 20,000 calls from domestic violence hotlines each day (National Coalition Against Domestic Violence fact sheet). However, many victims suffer in silence, never reaching out for help.

Country-wise statistics on domestic violence against men:

United States:

While domestic violence is frequently associated with female victims, research shows that men are also subjected to signif-icant levels of abuse. Approximately one in every four men in the United States will experience some form of intimate partner violence (IPV) in their lifetime. 43% of men report experiencing psychological aggression from their intimate partner (Domestic Violence Research Law Office of Louis J. Goodman).

United Kingdom:

In England and Wales, approximately 786,000 men were victims of domestic abuse during the fiscal year ending March 2020. This accounts for approximately 3.8% of men aged 16 to 59 (Domestic Violence Research).

Australia:

Australian statistics indicate that one in six men has experienced emotional abuse by a current or previous partner since the age of 15. According to data from Australia's National Research Organization for Women's Safety (ANROWS), one out of every 16 men has been subjected to physical or sexual violence by a current or former partner (Domestic Violence Research).

Canada:

In Canada, Statistics Canada reports that approximately 5% of men reported being victims of spousal violence in the last five years, with rates for men being comparable to those for women—domestic violence research.

India:

India has lower rates of domestic violence against men. According to a study conducted by the Save Indian Family Foundation (SIFF), a men's rights organization in India, 51.5% of Indian men have experienced physical, emotional, or psychological abuse from their wives. These incidents include verbal threats, psychological manipulation, and physical assault.

New Zealand:

According to a study conducted by New Zealand's Ministry of Justice, 29% of men have experienced some form of intimate partner violence (IPV) in their lifetime, which can include physical, psychological, or sexual abuse. This figure reflects a widespread problem in the country, affecting men from various social classes.

Ireland:

According to a survey by the National Crime Council and the Economic and Social Research Institute, 6% of men reported experiencing severe abuse from their partner at some point in their lives, including physical, emotional, and sexual abuse—domestic violence research.

South Africa:

A study by the South African Medical Research Council found

that approximately 20% of men reported experiencing emotional abuse from their partners. In comparison, 10% reported physical abuse—domestic violence research.

Germany:

According to data from the German Federal Ministry for Family Affairs, approximately 19% of men have experienced domestic violence, including physical and psychological abuse, at some point in their lives.

Sweden:

From the statistics, according to Swedish research, approximately 8% of men aged 18-74 have experienced domestic violence, which includes physical violence, threats, and sexual violence from a current or former partner.

Denmark:

Domestic violence against men is becoming increasingly prevalent in Denmark. According to the Danish National Centre for Social Research, approximately 22% of men have suffered physical, emotional, or psychological abuse from a current or former partner at some point in their lives.

France:

France now recognizes domestic violence against men. According to the National Institute of Statistics and Economic Studies (INSEE), 4% of men aged 18 to 75 have experienced physical or sexual violence from a partner at least once in their lives.

Russia:

Data on domestic violence against men in Russia is difficult to obtain due to cultural stigmas and limited reporting. However, a report by the Moscow Helsinki Group suggested that approximately 10% of men in Russia had experienced domestic abuse, though the actual figure is likely under reported due to solid societal norms that discourage men from coming forward.

Japan:

In Japan, there is a growing awareness of domestic violence against men. According to a survey conducted by the Japanese Cabinet Office, approximately 13% of men have experienced some form of abuse from their partner, whether emotional, financial, or physical, in their lifetime.

These statistics show that domestic violence against men is a worldwide problem, with significant variations in prevalence rates between regions. This highlights the importance of inclusive policies and support systems that acknowledge and address the experiences of male victims of domestic violence.

Through this chapter, we aim to spark a broader understanding of the hidden epidemic of domestic violence against men and the importance of breaking the silence that surrounds it. This global issue demands global attention, inclusive support systems, and a compassionate understanding of the suffering that so many men endure.

Chapter 4: The Gender Bias in Domestic Violence Laws

Men and women are classified as human beings; hence, human rights should apply to all genders. Surprisingly, specific laws in most countries do not expressly mention this. A casual look at several such laws demonstrates that the law does not consider males to be human.

Some countries' present domestic violence laws do not acknowledge the idea of men becoming victims. Domestic violence is frequently perceived in society as something committed by husbands against wives. However, the unfortunate harsh reality is that even spouses commit domestic abuse against their husbands.

Marriage is commonly viewed as a union characterized by love, companionship, and mutual support. However, the reality can sometimes differ from this ideal. Many men suffer in silence from the difficulties of a troubled marriage, dealing with emotional turmoil and psychological stress in the absence of a support system or an outlet for their emotions.

Consider the case of David, a successful professional in his early 40s trapped in a marriage that gradually drained his spirit. Emily, David's wife, had become more critical and demanding over time. Minor disagreements became ongoing arguments, leaving David feeling inadequate and emotionally exhausted. He found himself walking on eggshells, attempting to avoid conflict but never succeeding. His once vibrant personality was overshadowed by anxiety and self-doubt.

David's story is familiar. Many men find themselves in similar situations, with their marriage dynamics shifting, leaving them feeling trapped and powerless. These men frequently suffer in silence, fearing that expressing their problems would make them appear weak or incapable. Society's expectations add to the burden, implying that men must always be strong and stoic.

David's path to healing began when he acknowledged his problems and sought assistance. He learned to **establish boundaries, effectively communicate his needs, and rebuild his self-esteem**. This transformation did not occur overnight. However, with patience and perseverance, David discovered a way to a healthier and more fulfilling marriage.

Using David's story, for instance, there is hope and guidance for those who are feeling lost in their marriages. Just remember that seeking help and working toward a better relationship does not indicate weakness; it demonstrates your strength and commitment to creating a better life for yourself and your family.

As you continue to the next chapter, I encourage you to think about your experiences and how to apply these strategies to your current situation. You are not alone in this journey, and with the right support, you will overcome the obstacles and find your way to peace and fulfillment.

Chapter 5: Identifying Problematic Behaviors

motional manipulation often includes extreme tactics like threatening suicide to control a partner's actions and emotions. This manipulation leverages fear, guilt, and obligation to maintain power in the relationship. Unfortunately, some individuals—both men and women—may use threats of self-harm or suicide to coerce their partners into compliance or to prevent them from making decisions that conflict with the manipulator's desires.

In a marital context, this behavior can place immense emotional pressure on the partner being manipulated, as they may feel responsible for the manipulator's well-being. Such threats are not only emotionally damaging but also dangerous, as they undermine healthy communication and mutual respect in the relationship.

Emotional manipulation:

Emotional manipulation is a subtle but effective tactic in which a wife controls or influences her husband's emotions to her advantage. This behavior could include guilt-tripping, playing the victim, or using affection to control his actions.

Signs of Emotional Manipulation:

- Guilt Tripping: She makes him feel guilty for expressing his needs, making him appear selfish.
- Victimhood: She often blames him for her happiness or failures.
- Using Vulnerabilities: She manipulates his decisions by leveraging his weaknesses and personal insecurities.

How To Recognize And Document:

- Maintain a journal. Record instances of emotional manipulation, such as dates, conversations, and feelings.
- Seek external validation: Discuss your experience with a trusted friend or therapist to validate your emotions.
- Record conversations: If legal, document instances of apparent manipulation to gain clarity.

Gaslighting:

Gaslighting is a severe form of manipulation in which your wife causes you to doubt your reality. It can gradually erode your self-esteem and sense of reality.

Signs of Gaslighting:

- Denial of Events: She denies conversations or incidents you recall.

- Accusations of Paranoia: When confronted, she accuses you of being overly sensitive and paranoid.
- Twisting Truth: She alters facts to challenge your judgment and memory.

How to Recognize and Document:

- Write Things Down: Record conversations, events, and her responses.
- Speak with Trusted Sources: Seek a third-party perspective to validate your experiences.
- Record Proof: Safely record confrontations or situations to review later.

Excessive control and dominance:

A wife who exerts excessive control reduces her husband's autonomy, resulting in dependency and fear. This behavior frequently involves controlling how he spends his time and money and who he can associate with.

Signs of Excessive Control:

- Dictating life choices: She controls your time, money, and social interactions.
- She closely monitors your phone, emails, and location.
- Loss of Autonomy: Major decisions are made without input, leaving you powerless.

How to Recognize And Document:

- Log moments of excessive control.
- Establish boundaries and communicate your need for more freedom.
- Seek support from others who can provide advice and emotional strength.

Constant Criticism and Belittling:

Constant criticism and belittling damage self-esteem. If your wife frequently discredits your abilities and decisions, you may begin to feel worthless.

Signs of Criticism and Belittling:

- Derogatory Remarks: She regularly makes negative comments about your actions or choices.
- No Praise: There is rarely, if ever, positive reinforcement or acknowledgment.
- Never Good Enough: You constantly fail to meet her expectations.

How to Recognize and Document:

- Track the Patterns: Write down instances of criticism and note the patterns.
- Communicate Your Feelings: Let her know how her words make you feel and request constructive feedback.
- Build Self-Worth: Engage in activities that boost your confidence and remind you of your strengths.

Emotional unavailability and neglect:

An emotionally unavailable or neglectful wife causes her husband to feel isolated and disconnected. This type of neglect can be equally harmful as more overt forms of abuse.

Signs of Emotional Unavailability:

- Lack of Emotional Expression: She rarely expresses or discusses her emotions.

- She dismisses your requests for emotional connection or support.
- Feeling of isolation: Despite physical presence, you feel emotionally disconnected.

How to Recognize and Document:

- Journal Your Emotions: Identify times when you feel emotionally neglected.
- Encourage open communication about feelings.
- Seek emotional support from friends, family, or a therapist.

Financial Control and Abuse

A wife who controls the finances creates dependency, restricting your access to money and limiting your freedom.

Signs of Financial Control:

- Restricted Access: She limits your access to joint accounts or financial information.
- Monitoring Spending: She controls your spending and demands to know how every penny is used.
- Blocking Income: She discourages or prevents you from earning your own money.

How to Recognize and Document:

- Track Financial Restrictions: Document how your access to finances is restricted or controlled.

- Educate Yourself: Gain financial literacy and understand your rights.
- Seek Legal Advice: Consult a lawyer about your financial rights and options.

Types of Difficult Wives and Their Abnormal Behaviors

Understanding specific behavioral types can help men better identify the root causes of distress in their marriages.

1. The Controlling Wife:

- Traits: Micromanages her husband's life, isolates him from others, and exerts financial control.
- Behavior Example: A man whose wife controls every aspect of his daily life, from social interactions to finances, faces her wrath if he tries to assert his independence.

2. The Manipulative Wife:

- Traits: Uses gaslighting, emotional blackmail, and victim-playing to keep her husband dependent.
- Behavior Example: A husband constantly apologizes for things he didn't do, doubting his reality because his wife twists every truth.

3. The Passive-Aggressive Wife:

- Traits: Avoids confrontation, punishing her husband through silent treatment or sarcasm.
- Behavior Example: A wife who "forgets" requests or responds with biting sarcasm, making her husband frustrated and confused.

4. The Revenge-Seeking Wife:

- Traits: Causes harm to her husband by acting out of jealousy or perceived wrongdoing.
- Behavior Example: a wife who harms her husband's reputation and feelings by fabricating stories or influencing court cases.

5. The Unhappy Wife:

- Traits: Cheats or seeks attention outside the marriage due to dissatisfaction, using infidelity as a form of revenge.
- Behavior Example: An emotionally detached wife finds validation in another relationship, which causes pain in her marriage.

Recognizing problem behaviors in your marriage is the first step toward healing. Men who document and acknowledge these patterns can devise strategies to regain control of their mental and emotional health. Setting boundaries and seeking help are critical steps toward breaking the cycle of silent suffering. Men can use awareness to transform troubled relationships into healthier dynamics.

Cultural patterns of toxic behavior in marriages: A global perspective on difficult wives. The types of toxic wives or challenging behaviors observed in marriages vary depending on cultural expectations, societal norms, and gender dynamics in various countries. These behaviors are not limited to specific countries but can manifest differently depending on the cultural context.

overview of how toxic wife behavior may be perceived in different regions:

United States (or other Western countries): The "Controlling Wife"

- Controlling wives in Western cultures tend to be overly dominant in decision-making and micromanage their husbands' lives, careers, and social relationships. Financial control can also be a significant issue, with some wives denying their husbands access to joint accounts or making financial decisions.
- Western societies prioritize individualism and equality. When control becomes excessive, it undermines the ideal of a collaborative partnership.
- Common examples include excessive control over finances, social interactions, and emotional manipulation using guilt or blame.

India (South Asia): The "Traditional Manipulator"

- Toxic wives in India may use their solid societal and familial ties to exert control over their husbands. She could also use emotional blackmail by involving the extended family in personal matters.
- In traditional Indian households, societal and familial expectations greatly impact marital relationships. Toxic wives may use the traditional family hierarchy to shape the narrative.
- Common examples include threats to a family's reputation or using children as leverage in disputes.

Middle East: The "Social Status Seeker"

- Toxic wives in certain Middle Eastern cultures may manipulate their husbands' careers or family connections to gain social status. She may also pressure him to meet unrealistic material or societal expectations.
- Toxic wives may exploit their culture's high value of social reputation and family honor.
- Common examples include applying cultural or societal norms to control a husband's actions or pressuring him for extravagant lifestyle changes.

Japan (East Asia): The "Emotionally Distant Wife"

- In Japan, toxic wives may exhibit emotional coldness, distance, or passive-aggressive behavior. She may refuse to engage emotionally with her husband, frequently withholding affection as punishment or control.
- Toxic wives may exploit the culture's emphasis on stoicism and emotional restraint, leading to emotional distance or

dismissive behavior.

· Common examples include silent treatment, emotional neglect, or using passive aggression to gain control in relationships.

Africa: The "Wife Who Exploits Patriarchal Norms"

· Toxic wives in Africa may use patriarchal norms like marriage, dowry, and family honor to control or degrade their

husbands.
- The strong emphasis on traditional gender roles can some-times be exploited by toxic wives who may use community or family pressures to assert dominance.
- Common examples include publicly shaming the husband, withholding emotional support, or manipulating social networks to isolate him.

Russia (Eastern Europe): The "Narcissistic Wife"

- A narcissistic wife in Russia may use her charm and wit to manipulate her husband emotionally and financially. She may belittle him publicly or privately to maintain her perceived superiority and control over the marriage.
- They may exploit societal pressures, especially in social or economic contexts, despite their culture's emphasis on family unity.
- Common examples include constant criticism, belittlement, and public humiliation.

Latin America – The "Jealous and Possessive Wife"

- In Latin America, where passionate, emotional expression is culturally familiar, a toxic wife might display excessive jealousy and possessiveness, often invading her husband's privacy and restricting his social interactions.
- Relationships in Latin America are often passionate, and jealousy can sometimes be interpreted as love. However, toxic jealousy can lead to extreme control and monitoring of the husband's activities.
- Common examples include checking the husband's phone

constantly, being suspicious of friendships with other women, and publicly accusing him of infidelity without cause.

China (East Asia) – The "Materialistic Wife"

- In modern Chinese society, where status and wealth are increasingly valued, a toxic wife may demand excessive material wealth and social status. She may measure her husband's financial worth by his ability to provide and pressure him to meet ever-increasing standards.
- As China has rapidly modernized, material success has become a key indicator of social status, which a toxic wife may exploit to place unreasonable demands on her husband.
- Common examples are demanding luxury goods, prioritizing social standing over emotional connection, or dismissing the husband's emotional needs.

Italy (Southern Europe): The "Overly Dependent Wife"

- In some parts of Italy, traditional family values prioritize a nurturing yet dependent role for women. A toxic wife may take this to an extreme, expecting her husband to meet all of her needs without reciprocation. She may become overly reliant on her husband emotionally, financially, and socially, refusing to contribute to their relationship.
- Italy's emphasis on family can lead to excessive dependency, resulting in an imbalanced relationship.
- Common examples include needing constant attention or emotional support, neglecting personal responsibilities, and relying on her husband's resources.

Philippines (Southeast Asia) – The "Manipulative Martyr"

- In the Philippines, where familial duty and sacrifice are cultural values, a toxic wife might manipulate these values by portraying herself as a long-suffering martyr. She may constantly remind her husband of her sacrifices, using guilt to control him.
- The Filipino culture highly values family and sacrifice, and this can be twisted by a toxic wife who uses self-pity and guilt to dominate the relationship.
- Common examples include reminding the husband of past sacrifices, exaggerating hardships for emotional leverage, or refusing to compromise.

Germany (Western Europe): The "Perfectionist Wife"

- In Germany, where efficiency and order are valued, a toxic wife may be overly critical of her husband's perceived failure to meet high standards. She may constantly nag, micromanage, and criticize her husband, making him feel inadequate.
- Toxic wives may demand perfection in all aspects of the relationship and household, contrary to German cultural values.
- Common examples include constantly pointing out flaws, failing to acknowledge her husband's efforts, and setting unrealistic expectations for the household.

Nigeria (West Africa) – The "Power Seeker"

- Toxic wives in Nigeria may use their position in the marriage to gain social or financial power. She may use her husband's connections to advance her career or exploit family resources for personal gain without regard for the relationship.

- Toxic wives may benefit from Nigerian culture's emphasis on status, wealth, and extended family ties.
- Common examples include using family ties for personal gain, controlling family resources, or utilizing her husband's connections to enhance her social standing.

Brazil (South America) – The "Drama Queen"

- In Brazil, where emotional expression is culturally familiar, a toxic wife may escalate minor issues into dramatic conflicts. She might use emotional outbursts to manipulate her husband or get her way, creating a rollercoaster of emotions in the relationship.
- Brazilian culture embraces emotional expressiveness, but in a toxic relationship, this can become excessive, leading to volatility and manipulation.
- Common examples include emotional manipulation through outbursts, creating unnecessary drama in daily interactions, or exaggerating problems to gain sympathy.

South Korea (East Asia) – The "Social Climber Wife"

- In South Korea, where social status and appearances are highly valued, a toxic wife may pressure her husband to achieve higher status, often by overworking or constantly comparing him to others. She might demand luxury goods or a lavish lifestyle to maintain social standing.

- South Korean society places significant emphasis on social status, wealth, and appearances, and a toxic wife might use these values to pressure her husband into overworking or living beyond their means.
- Common examples include constant demands for luxury items, pressuring the husband to achieve higher social status, and emphasizing appearances over genuine connection.

France (Western Europe): The "Emotionally Dismissive Wife"

- Toxic wives in France may exhibit emotional aloofness or dismissiveness, which is common in a culture that values intellect and independence. She may disregard her husband's emotional needs and refuse to engage in meaningful communication.
- Toxic wives in French culture may prioritize intellectual independence and emotional restraint, leading to avoidance of emotional intimacy or dismissal of concerns.
- Common examples include avoiding difficult conversations, minimizing her husband's emotional needs, or creating emotional distance to maintain control.

While these characteristics exist worldwide, cultural norms and expectations shape how they manifest. Each country has its own set of gender dynamics, societal pressures, and familial structures that contribute to the various types of toxicity observed in marriages. It's important to note that toxic behaviors can occur in any relationship, regardless of location, and addressing them necessitates awareness, communication, and, in some cases, external support.

Chapter 6: The Psychological Impact on Men

The sufferings of men under challenging marriages go far beyond the immediate emotional turmoil. Their spouses' problematic behaviors can have severe and long-term consequences for their mental well-being. In this chapter, we will look at how these behaviors affect men psychologically, the cycle of self-doubt, anxiety, and depression that they frequently experience, the impact on their self-esteem and self-worth, and the critical importance of acknowledging and addressing emotional distress.

How These Behaviors Affect Men's Mental Health

Emotional manipulation, excessive control, constant criticism, emotional neglect, and financial abuse all hurt men's mental health. These behaviors can result in a variety of psychological issues, including:

- Living in an emotionally abusive environment can cause chronic stress as the body and mind are constantly on high alert. This can cause physical symptoms like headaches, fatigue, and gastrointestinal problems, as well as mental health problems like anxiety and depression.

- Controlling behavior by a spouse can lead to isolation and loss of social support networks for men. This isolation can amplify feelings of loneliness and despair.
- Constantly navigating a minefield of manipulation and criticism leaves men emotionally drained. This emotional exhaustion makes it difficult to cope with daily life and can lead to burnout.

The Cycle of Self-Doubt, Anxiety, and Depression

The insidious nature of emotional abuse frequently traps men in this cycle.

- Constant criticism and gaslighting can lead to self-doubt. He begins to question his reality, including his worth and abilities. This self-doubt makes him vulnerable to further manipulation and control.
- Living in an emotionally volatile environment can lead to constant anxiety. Men become hypervigilant, waiting for the next outburst or criticism. This anxiety can cause restlessness, irritability, and difficulty concentrating.
- Chronic emotional abuse and isolation can lead to depression. Men may feel hopeless, lose interest in previously enjoyed activities, and experience feelings of worthlessness.
- In severe cases, this depression can lead to suicidal thoughts.

Impact on Self-Esteem and Self-Worth

A man's self-esteem and self-worth are particularly vulnerable to the effects of emotional abuse. The constant barrage of negative comments, belittling, and control can make him feel unworthy and incapable. This erosion of self-esteem manifests in several ways:

- **Negative Self-Image:** Men begin to see themselves through the critical lens of their abusive spouse. They internalize the negative messages, believing they are inherently flawed or unlovable.
- **Learned Helplessness:** Repeatedly experiencing situations where their efforts to assert themselves are met with hostility or manipulation can lead men to feel powerless. They

may start to believe that they have no control over their circumstances, leading to a sense of helplessness.

- **Fear of Failure:** The fear of further criticism or punishment can paralyze men, preventing them from taking risks or pursuing personal goals. This fear stifles their growth and contributes to a stagnant, unfulfilling life.

The Importance of Acknowledging and Addressing Emotional Pain:

Recognizing and addressing emotional pain is an essential step toward recovery and reclaiming one's life. Men must realize that their suffering is genuine and valid and that seeking help is not a sign of weakness but rather a brave act of self-care.

- **Breaking the Silence:** Sharing personal experiences can be highly liberating. Men who share their stories with trusted friends, family members, or support groups feel more understood and less alone. This also challenges societal norms that marginalize male vulnerability.
- **Seeking Professional Help:** Therapy and counseling offer a safe space for men to express emotions, gain insights, and develop coping strategies. Mental health professionals can assist men in rebuilding their self-esteem and creating a plan for the future.
- **Building Resilience:** Emotional resilience involves learning to manage stress, practicing self-compassion, and setting

healthy boundaries. Resilience enables men to navigate future challenges with greater confidence and strength.

- **Fostering Self-Worth**: Engaging in activities that nurture self-worth is essential for recovery. This can include pursuing hobbies, setting personal goals, and surrounding oneself with supportive and positive influences.

Chapter 7: Children: The Secondary Victims of Domestic Violence

Domestic violence is a widespread problem that affects more than just the primary victims, who are usually women or men. One of the most heartbreaking aspects of this violence is the effect it has on the children who witness it. Children in households where domestic violence occurs are frequently referred to as "secondary victims." Despite not being direct targets of violence, these children suffer profound and long-term psychological, emotional, and sometimes physical consequences.

The Impact on Children: Psychological and Emotional Effects

Children who witness domestic violence frequently develop a variety of psychological and emotional problems. According to studies, these children are more likely to develop anxiety, depression, and post-traumatic stress disorder (PTSD). Constant exposure to conflict and violence can cause chronic stress, which hurts brain development. Children may develop heightened levels of fear and anxiety, making them hyper-vigilant and overly cautious in their daily lives.

Furthermore, witnessing domestic violence can undermine a child's sense of safety and security. The home, which should be a haven, becomes a source of fear and uncertainty. Insecurity can lead to behaviors like withdrawal, aggression, sleep disturbances, and difficulty concentrating in school.

Behavioral and Social Consequences

These children frequently display behavioral issues such as aggression, delinquency, and defiance. These behaviors often reflect the confusion and turmoil they experience internally. They may mimic the abusive behavior they have witnessed, believing it is the usual way to interact with others. This can make it difficult to form healthy relationships and perpetuate a cycle of violence in the future.

Socially, these children may struggle to integrate with their peers. The stigma and shame associated with domestic violence can make them feel isolated, and they may struggle to trust others. They may also feel responsible for the violence, which can result in guilt and low self-esteem.

Academic Impact

Domestic violence frequently hurts children's academic performance. The stress and trauma of living in a violent household can impair cognitive functions, making it difficult for children to focus, retain information, and succeed in school. They may also miss school more frequently due to domestic chaos or because they are dealing with the psychological consequences of the violence.

Physical Health Implications

The physical health of children exposed to domestic violence is also at risk. Chronic exposure to stress can weaken their immune system, making them more susceptible to illnesses. Additionally, children in these environments are more likely to suffer physical injuries, either from being directly involved in the violence or from neglect. They may also engage in risky behaviors, such as substance abuse, as a way to cope with their environment.

Long-Term Consequences

The long-term consequences of being a secondary victim of domestic violence can last into adulthood. These people are more likely to develop mental health problems, such as depression and anxiety, throughout their lifetime. They may also struggle with relationship issues, frequently repeating abusive behaviors they witnessed as children. If not addressed, the cycle of violence can continue for generations.

Additionally, adults who grew up in violent households may struggle to regulate their emotions and manage stress. They may also face parenting challenges, such as becoming overly permissive or excessively strict to avoid replicating the abusive environment they experienced as children.

Numerous studies have examined the prevalence and impact of domestic violence on children. According to the National Child Traumatic Stress Network, approximately 15.5 million children in the United States live in households with domestic violence. The World Health Organization reports that domestic violence affects up to 275 million children worldwide each year.

According to research, children who have experienced domestic violence are six times more likely to commit suicide, 50% more likely to abuse drugs and alcohol, and 74% more likely to commit a violent crime against another person. These statistics highlight the critical importance of intervention and support for these children.

Intervention in the lives of children who are secondary victims of domestic violence is critical to breaking the cycle of abuse. Early intervention programs that offer psychological support, safe environments, and educational resources can significantly improve the lives of these children. It is also critical to address the needs of the entire family by providing resources and support to both the victim and the perpetrator of violence to create a safer home environment.

This chapter serves as a reminder that domestic violence is a societal issue affecting our communities' most vulnerable members. Several solutions can be used to reduce the adverse effects of domestic violence on children. These interventions are intended to provide children and families with emotional support, safety, and educational resources.

Here are a few critical approaches:

1. Offer trauma-informed counseling.

Children who have been victims of domestic violence frequently require psychological support to help them cope. Trauma-informed counseling can help them develop healthy coping mechanisms, manage anxiety, and avoid internalizing guilt or fear. For younger children, play therapy and art therapy are effective. In contrast, older children may benefit from one-on-one sessions with a licensed therapist. Family therapy provides an opportunity to meet the emotional needs of the entire family.

Working with a trained therapist can help families learn better ways to interact and resolve conflict. Mediation may also help to reduce tension between parents and improve communication, reducing children's exposure to harmful behaviors.

2. Create a safe space.

Ensuring that children have a safe and secure environment is essential. Suppose the home is unsafe due to ongoing violence. Other options, such as shelters, foster care, or staying with extended family, may be required. Schools, community centers, and other organizations can provide safe spaces for children to express themselves without fear of being judged or punished.

The school where the children attend plays a crucial role as they can be a valuable resource for these children. Teachers and counselors should be trained to recognize signs of domestic violence and offer assistance. Schools can also provide access to mental health professionals, after-school programs, and academic support to help children succeed despite obstacles at home.

3. Implement early intervention programs.

Early intervention programs in schools and communities can help children learn about healthy relationships, emotional regulation, and conflict resolution. These programs not only assist children who are currently victims of domestic violence but also help to prevent future violence by educating the next generation about healthy behaviors.

4. Parental Support and Education

Supporting parents, both victims and perpetrators of domestic violence, is critical. Rehabilitation programs that focus on anger management, conflict resolution, and breaking the cycle of violence can help perpetrators. Victims can regain control of their lives by participating in support groups and seeking counseling. Addressing parental well-being can significantly reduce the risk of violence against children.

5. Law and Policy Advocacy

Laws should ensure that children in violent households have adequate protection and access to mental health services. Mandatory reporting of child exposure to domestic violence can help authorities intervene sooner, giving children early access to assistance. Policies, when created, should be made known to the public as raising public awareness about the effects of domestic violence on children can encourage more proactive community involvement. Educational campaigns can focus on dispelling myths, such as the notion that domestic violence only affects adult victims, and emphasize the importance of addressing children's experiences as secondary victims.

Chapter 8: Strategies for Emotional Resilience

When faced with emotional and psychological challenges in a difficult marriage, men must develop emotional resilience to navigate their unhealthy situation and reclaim their well-being. Emotional resilience is the ability to adapt and recover from adversity, rebound stronger from setbacks, and maintain a positive outlook in the face of life's challenges. This chapter delves into various techniques and practices that can assist men in developing emotional resilience, establishing a strong sense of self, and prioritizing self-care and personal wellness.

Techniques for Developing Emotional Resilience

Building emotional resilience entails developing habits and mindsets to manage stress, overcome adversity, and maintain a balanced perspective. Here are a few effective techniques:

Prioritize positive aspects of your life and express gratitude. Keep a journal and write down what you are grateful for every day. This helps you shift your focus away from problems and toward possibilities.

Flexibility: Learn to adapt to changing circumstances. Accept change as an opportunity for growth rather than a threat.

Improve your problem-solving skills by breaking down problems into manageable steps. Approach challenges methodically and look for solutions rather than dwelling on the issue.

Establish and maintain strong relationships with friends, family, and support groups. Having a support system provides emotional support and practical advice during difficult times.

Maintain an optimistic mindset by visualizing positive outcomes and focusing on what you can control. Believe in your ability to overcome challenges.

Mindfulness and Meditation Practices

Mindfulness and meditation are powerful practices for staying grounded, managing stress, and developing emotional resilience. They include paying attention to the present moment, acknowledging your thoughts and feelings without judgment, and cultivating a sense of calm and clarity.

Set aside time daily to practice mindfulness meditation. Sit quietly, concentrate on breathing, and notice your thoughts and sensations without attempting to change them. This practice helps to reduce stress and improve emotional regulation.

Body Scan Meditation:

To practice Body Scan Meditation, lie in a comfortable position and focus on different body parts, beginning with your toes and progressing to your head. Recognize any tension or discomfort and breathe into it to relieve stress.

Loving-Kindness Meditation:

Practice compassion and empathy by silently repeating phrases like "May I be happy, healthy, and safe" for yourself and others. This practice can boost feelings of connectedness while reducing negative emotions.

Mindful Breathing:

Throughout the day, take breaks to focus on your breathing. Inhale deeply and exhale slowly, focusing on the sensation of the breath entering and leaving your body. This simple practice can quickly relieve stress and return you to the present moment.

Developing a Strong Sense of Self

Emotional resilience requires a strong sense of self. Understanding your values, strengths, and identity is critical, as is remaining honest and authentic in your actions and decisions.

Regularly consider your values, beliefs, and goals. Understand what's important to you and how you want to live. Journaling can be an effective tool for this process.

Establish personal goals. Set short—and long-term goals—that align with your values and passions. Working toward these goals provides a sense of purpose and direction.

Embrace your strengths. Recognize and celebrate your strengths and achievements. Focus on your strengths and use them to overcome challenges.

Assertiveness Training: Develop clear and confident communication skills for your needs, desires, and boundaries. Assertiveness allows you to maintain your sense of self while respecting others.

The Role of Self-Care and Personal Well-Being

Prioritizing self-care and personal well-being is critical for developing and sustaining emotional resilience. Self-care entails intentionally protecting your physical, mental, and emotional health.

Maintain physical health by exercising regularly, eating well, and getting enough sleep. Physical health is closely related to emotional well-being.

Prioritize mental health by engaging in stimulating and enjoyable activities. This could include reading, learning new skills, or engaging in hobbies that you are passionate about.

Improve emotional health by practicing self-compassion and kindness. Allow yourself to experience and process your emotions without judgment. Seek professional help if needed.

Relaxation techniques: Incorporate relaxation techniques into your daily activities. Deep breathing exercises, progressive muscle relaxation, and spending time in nature are all possible options.

Establish and maintain healthy boundaries to ensure your well-being. This includes limiting your time, energy, and resources and saying no when necessary.

While much has been said, developing emotional resilience necessitates dedication and practice.

Chapter 9: Effective Communication Techniques

Communication is the foundation of any relationship; it fosters understanding, trust, and conflict resolution. For men in challenging marriages, mastering effective communication techniques is critical for addressing issues, expressing needs, and cultivating a healthier, more supportive partnership. This chapter discusses the importance of communication in conflict resolution and how to express feelings. It needs assertive, active listening, empathetic responses, and strategies for defusing arguments and de-escalating tension.

The Importance of Communication in Resolving Conflicts

Effective communication is critical for conflict resolution and maintaining a healthy relationship. When partners can openly and honestly share their thoughts, feelings, and concerns, misunderstandings are reduced, and mutual understanding improves. Poor communication frequently exacerbates issues in challenging marriages, increasing frustration, resentment, and emotional distance.

- Open communication prevents conflicts by clarifying misunderstandings and assumptions.
- Consistent, honest communication promotes trust and security in relationships.
- Regularly sharing thoughts and feelings between partners strengthens their emotional connection.
- Effective communication enables partners to resolve issues collaboratively, resulting in mutually beneficial solutions.

How to Express Feelings and Needs Assertively

Assertive communication entails expressing your thoughts, feelings and needs clearly and respectfully without becoming aggressive or passive. It allows you to stand up for yourself while still respecting your partner.

- Use "I" statements. Begin sentences with "I" to emphasize your emotions and avoid sounding accusatory. Say, "I feel hurt when..." rather than "You always..."
- Be specific: Clearly articulate your needs or desires, using particular examples. Instead of saying, "You never help around the house," state, "I need help with the dishes after dinner."
- Maintain a calm and steady tone while discussing complex topics. This will help avoid escalation and keep the conversation productive.
- Practice Self-Awareness: Be aware of your emotions and take a moment to collect your thoughts before speaking. This ensures that you communicate effectively and thought-

fully.

Active Listening and Empathetic Responses

Active listening is an essential part of effective communication. It entails entirely focusing on the speaker, understanding their message, and responding thoughtfully. Empathetic responses demonstrate that you value your partner's emotions and perspectives.

- Focus on your partner: Avoid distractions and pay full attention when they speak. Make eye contact and demonstrate attentiveness.
- Reflect: To ensure you understand, paraphrase what your partner said: "It sounds like you're feeling frustrated because..."
- Ask questions: Show interest by asking open-ended questions that prompt your partner to elaborate. Let's say: "Can you tell me more about how that made you feel?"
- Validate Feelings: Acknowledge and validate your partner's emotions, even if you don't entirely agree. For example, "I understand you're upset, and I appreciate you sharing that with me."
- Avoid Interrupting: Allow your partner to speak without interruption. Wait until they have finished before responding.

Strategies for Defusing Arguments and DE-Escalating Tension

Conflict is unavoidable in any relationship, but how you manage it can make a big difference. Strategies to defuse arguments and DE-escalate tension can help prevent disputes from spiraling out of control.

- If emotions are high, take a timeout to calm down before continuing the conversation. Set a specific time to resume the discussion.
- Stay focused on the issue and avoid bringing up past grievances or unrelated topics.
- Maintain a calm tone, even if your partner becomes agitated. This helps to avoid further escalation.
- Acknowledge and sincerely apologize for any mistakes. Taking responsibility can help to reduce tension.

Find Common Ground: Look for points of agreement and build on them. Finding common ground can shift the focus away from conflict and towards collaboration.

Agree to Disagree: It's acceptable to disagree. Recognize that it is sufficient for you and your partner to have different points of view.

Chapter 10: Setting Boundaries and Reclaiming Control

Setting and maintaining healthy boundaries under challenging marriages is critical for protecting your well-being and regaining control of your life. Boundaries define acceptable and unacceptable, ensuring that both partners respect each other's limitations and needs. This chapter discusses the significance of setting healthy boundaries, how to set and maintain them effectively, how to deal with resistance and push back from a problematic spouse, and how to reclaim control of your life and decisions.

The Importance of Setting Healthy Boundaries

Healthy boundaries are essential for any relationship to thrive. They provide a framework for mutual respect, trust, and understanding. In difficult marriages, setting boundaries is especially important for protecting yourself from emotional, psychological, and even physical harm.

- Setting boundaries demonstrates self-respect and awareness of one's own needs. It expresses that you value your well-being and expect the same from your partner.

- Boundaries prevent burnout by allowing time for self-care and personal interests.
- Respecting each other's boundaries builds trust and promotes a healthier, more balanced relationship.
- Boundaries promote autonomy and independence, allowing partners to pursue their goals.
-

How to Set and Maintain Boundaries Effectively

Setting and maintaining boundaries requires clear communication, consistency, and self-awareness. Here are some steps to help you set and maintain your boundaries effectively:

- Identify your needs. Consider your values, needs, and limits. Understand what is non-negotiable for your health and happiness.
- Express your boundaries to your spouse clearly, concisely, and respectfully. Use "I" statements to emphasize your feelings and needs. For example, "I need time alone each day to recharge."
- Maintaining boundaries requires consistent behavior. Maintain your boundaries consistently to emphasize their significance. Allowing them to cross on occasion sends mixed messages.
- Enforce boundaries with appropriate consequences. This demonstrates that you are serious about staying within your limits.
- Revisit and adjust boundaries as your relationship evolves. Check in with yourself regularly to ensure your boundaries meet your needs.

Dealing with Resistance and Push back from a Difficult Spouse

When establishing boundaries in a difficult marriage, it is expected to face resistance or push back from your spouse. The changes may threaten or challenge them, prompting an adverse reaction. Here's how to deal with resistance effectively:

- Stay firm: Maintain your boundaries. Consistency is essential for learning to respect your boundaries.
- Demonstrate empathy by acknowledging your spouse's feelings and concerns. Use empathetic statements such as, "I understand how difficult this is for you, but it is necessary for my well-being."
- Remain Calm: Control your emotions and respond calmly to resistance. Reacting in anger or frustration can exacerbate the situation.
- Seek support from friends, family, or a therapist. Having a support system can help you remain strong.
- Educate Your Spouse: Help your spouse understand why these boundaries are necessary for your mental and emotional health. Share resources or suggest couples therapy to work on boundaries together.

Reclaiming Control Over Your Own Life and Decisions

Regaining control of your life and decisions entails taking proactive steps to assert your independence and prioritize your needs. Here's how you can regain control:

- Make self-care a top priority in your daily routine. Engage in activities that will benefit your mind, body, and spirit.
- Set personal goals that reflect your values and interests. Focusing on your goals, whether for a hobby, professional advancement, or personal development, can help you feel empowered.
- Improve Decision-Making Skills: Practice making decisions independently. Begin with small choices and gradually progress to larger ones. Believe in your judgment and instincts.
- Surround yourself with supportive, positive individuals who respect your boundaries and promote growth.
- Educate yourself on your legal and financial rights. This can help you make better decisions and feel more in control.
- Seek professional help: Therapy or counseling can help you gain insight into your situation and develop strategies to regain independence and control.

Chapter 11: Seeking Professional Help

Amid a problematic marriage, seeking professional help can be a game changer for healing and resolution. Therapy and counseling provide a safe environment for individuals and couples to explore their emotions, address underlying issues, and develop healthier communication strategies. This chapter discusses the role of therapy and counseling in dealing with difficult marriages, how to select the right therapist or counselor, the advantages of individual and couples therapy, and how to overcome the stigma of seeking professional assistance.

The Role of Therapy and Counseling in Dealing with Difficult Marriages

Therapy and counseling can help people navigate the complexities of difficult marriages. Professional therapists and counselors are trained to offer support, guidance, and tools for managing and resolving marital conflicts. They provide an objective viewpoint and a safe environment for discussing sensitive topics that would be difficult to address alone.

- Therapists offer objective insight, allowing partners to understand each other's perspectives better.
- Counselors assist couples in developing practical communication skills and conflict resolution strategies, allowing for constructive dispute resolution.
- Emotional Support: Therapy provides a safe space to express emotions and receive support. This can be especially important for men who may feel isolated.
- Identifying Patterns: Therapists can help identify negative behavior patterns and underlying issues contributing to marital difficulties, providing a pathway for change and growth.

How to Choose the Right Therapist or Counselor

Choosing the right therapist or counselor is critical to a successful therapeutic experience. Here are some steps to help you find a professional who fits your needs:

- Research credentials: Look for a licensed therapist or counselor who has relevant qualifications and experience with marital or relationship counseling. Professional associations, such as the American Association for Marriage and Family Therapy (AAMFT), can be valuable resources.
- Seek recommendations: Seek recommendations from friends, family, or your primary care physician. Personal referrals can provide valuable information about a therapist's approach and effectiveness.
- Interview potential therapists. Schedule initial consultations with several therapists to determine their compatibility. Inquire about their experience, therapeutic approach,

and how they handle situations like yours.

- Certain therapists specialize in specific areas, such as emotional abuse, communication issues, or infidelity. Finding a therapist who specializes in your particular challenges can be beneficial.
- Assess comfort level: It is crucial to feel at ease and safe with your therapist. Trust your instincts and choose someone with whom you have a positive rapport.

The Benefits of Individual and Couples Therapy

Both individual and couples therapy offers distinct benefits that can help you navigate a difficult marriage.

Individual Therapy:

- Personal Growth: Individual therapy focuses on one's personal experiences, emotions, and growth. It helps one understand one's feelings and behaviors and how they impact one's relationship.
- Developing Coping Strategies: A therapist can help you develop coping strategies for stress, anxiety, and other emotional challenges.
- Building Self-Esteem: Therapy can help rebuild your self-esteem and self-worth, which a problematic marriage may have eroded.
- Clarifying Goals: Individual therapy provides a space to define your personal and relational goals, helping you make informed decisions about your future.

Couples Therapy:

- Couples therapy improves communication by helping partners express their needs and listen to each other more effectively.
- A therapist can facilitate productive discussions to resolve conflicts and reach common ground.
- Couples therapy can improve trust and emotional intimacy, strengthening partners' connection.
- Therapists help couples find practical solutions to their issues and create a plan for positive change.
- Overcoming the Stigma of Seeking Professional Help

Despite the apparent benefits, seeking professional assistance can be difficult due to societal stigma and misunderstandings about therapy. Overcoming this stigma is critical for getting the help you need.

- Recognize the Need for Help: Seeking assistance is a sign of strength, not weakness. It demonstrates a desire to improve your well-being and relationship.
- Educate yourself and others on the benefits of therapy. Education can help to debunk myths and reduce stigma.
- Seek support from friends and family who have had positive experiences with therapy. Their support and understanding can help you take the first step.
- Normalize Therapy: Recognize that therapy is a popular and valuable strategy for dealing with various problems. Many people go to therapy to improve their relationships and lives.
- Pay Attention to the Positive Outcomes: Pay Attention

to the possible advantages and constructive adjustments that therapy may bring about. The promise of a happier, healthier life can overcome any hesitancy.

Seeking professional help is a significant step toward healing and improving a troubled marriage. Therapy and counseling provide helpful tools and support for overcoming complex emotional and relational challenges. Turn the page and let us continue our journey of understanding, resilience, and transformation together.

Chapter 12: Building a Support Network

H aving a solid support network is essential in the face of a difficult marriage. It offers emotional support, practical advice, and a sense of belonging, which can significantly impact resilience and well-being. This chapter discusses the value of having a support system, how to contact friends, family, and support groups, the role of online communities and forums, and finding strength and solidarity in shared experiences.

The Importance of Having a Strong Support System

A strong support network serves as a lifeline during difficult times. It gives you a safe place to express yourself, gain perspective, and be encouraged. A support network can help men navigate the complexities of a difficult marriage.

- Supportive friends and family provide emotional validation, reducing feelings of isolation.
- Trusted individuals can provide practical advice and solutions based on their experience or expertise.
- Support networks provide encouragement and motivation for positive change and healing.

- Friends and family can hold you accountable to your goals and commitments, keeping you on track.
- Stress Relief: Spending time with supportive people can reduce stress and provide a much-needed break from marital issues.

How to Reach Out to Friends, Family, and Support Groups

Reaching out for support can be daunting, especially when dealing with sensitive issues. However, opening up to trusted individuals can be crucial to healing.

- Identify Trusted Individuals: Consider those in your life who have demonstrated compassion, understanding, and reliability. These are the people who can offer genuine help.
- Communicate openly and honestly about your feelings and experiences. Explain your situation clearly, and express your need for assistance.
- Establish boundaries when seeking support, including what topics to discuss and the desired level of involvement from others.
- Join support groups. Look for local or online support groups for people in similar circumstances. These groups allow you to share your experiences and learn from others who understand your challenges.

The Role of Online Communities and Forums

Online communities and forums provide a unique opportunity

to connect with others with similar experiences. They offer anonymity, accessibility, and an abundance of collective knowledge.

- Anonymity and privacy: Online communities offer the option to share experiences and seek advice anonymously, reassuring those hesitant to share their situation with others.
- Online forums offer 24/7 support.
- Collaborating with individuals from diverse backgrounds and experiences can provide unique perspectives and solutions.
- Finding the Right Community: Search for forums or groups that address relationship issues, men's mental health, or emotional abuse. Ensure that the community is supportive and moderated to maintain a safe environment.

Finding Strength and Solidarity in Shared Experiences

Connecting with people who have faced similar challenges can be highly empowering. Shared experiences provide a sense of solidarity and remind you that you are not alone in your struggles.

- Shared Understanding: Connecting with others who have experienced similar situations can provide a unique sense of empathy and understanding.
- Learn from others' experiences to gain practical advice and inspiration for your journey.
- Sharing experiences can foster strong and supportive bonds,

forming a valuable support network.
- Encouraging Growth: Seeing others' progress and recovery can inspire personal growth and development.

Creating a support network is essential in navigating a problematic marriage and reclaiming your well-being. A robust support system formed by friends, family, support groups, or online communities provides emotional validation, practical advice, and a sense of belonging. Reaching out and connecting with others can help you find strength and solidarity in shared experiences, allowing you to face challenges with more resilience and hope.

Contact Information for Support Groups and Counseling Services by Country

This comprehensive list of resources and support services is designed to provide you with the help you need, no matter where you are.

USA:

The National Domestic Violence Hotline

- To contact the hotline, visit www.thehotline.org
- Or call 1-800-799-SAFE (7233).
- How to approach: Call or chat online for confidential help and resources.

American Psychological Association (APA)

- Website: www.apa.org
- How to Approach: Use the APA's Psychologist Locator to find a licensed therapist near you.

Men's Resource Center

- Website: www.menscenter.org
- How to Approach: Explore resources and support programs for men dealing with emotional and relational issues.

UK:

Men's Advice Line

- Website: www.mensadviceline.org.uk
- Phone: 0808 801 0327
- How to Approach: Call for confidential support or use the email and web chat options.

Relate

- Website: www.relate.org.uk
- How to Approach: Book counseling sessions online for relationship support and advice.

Mind

- Website: www.mind.org.uk
- How to Approach: Access mental health support resources

and find local support groups.

Australia:

Men's Line Australia

- Website: www.mensline.org.au
- Phone: 1300 78 99 78
- How to Approach: Call or use the online chat for confidential counseling and support.

Relationships Australia

- Website: www.relationships.org.au
- How to Approach: Find and book counseling services online.

Beyond Blue

- Website: www.beyondblue.org.au
- How to Approach: Access resources for mental health support and connect with online forums.

Canada:

Dawn House

- Website: www.dawnhouse.ca
- How to Approach: Access support services for men experiencing domestic abuse.

Canadian Mental Health Association (CMHA)

- Website: www.cmha.ca
- How to Approach: Find local CMHA branches for mental health support and services.

Family Services of Greater Vancouver

- Website: www.fsgv.ca
- How to Approach: Explore counseling and support services for individuals and families.

Italy:

Telefono Rosa

- Website: www.telefonorosa.it
- How to Approach: Contact for support in cases of domestic abuse and emotional support.

Psicologi Italia

- Website: www.psicologi-italia.it
- How to Approach: Find licensed psychologists and mental health professionals across Italy.

Centro di Ascolto Uomini Maltrattanti (CAM)

- Website: www.centrouominimaltrattanti.org
- How to Approach: Seek support specifically designed for men facing abuse.

New Zealand:

White Ribbon New Zealand

- Website: www.whiteribbon.org.nz
- How to Approach: Access resources for men and join community events and support groups.

Victim Support New Zealand

- Website: www.victimsupport.org.nz
- Phone: 0800 842 846
- How to Approach: Call for immediate support and find local support services.

Mental Health Foundation of New Zealand

- Website: www.mentalhealth.org.nz
- How to Approach: Explore mental health resources and find local support groups and services.

India:

Save Indian Family Foundation (SIFF)

- Website: www.saveindianfamily.org
- How to Approach: Access resources and support for men facing domestic issues, including legal assistance and counseling.

The Alternative Story

- Website: www.thealternativestory.in
- How to Approach: Book online counseling sessions for mental health support, including individual and couples therapy.

Manas Foundation

- Website: www.manas.org.in
- How to Approach: Explore mental health services and counseling options for emotional and psychological support.

Japan:

Tokyo Mental Health

- Website: www.tokyomentalhealth.com
- How to Approach: Book online appointments for counseling and therapy services.

TELL Japan

- Website: www.telljp.com
- Phone: 03-5774-0992
- How to Approach: Call the helpline for mental health support and counseling services or join their online support groups.

Japan Therapy Network

- Website: www.japantherapy.com
- How to Approach: Use the online directory to find therapists and counselors across Japan.

France:

SOS Hommes Battus

- Website: www.sos-hommes-battus.fr
- How to Approach: Access resources and support specifically for men experiencing domestic violence.

Psychologues Paris

- Website: www.psychologues-paris.fr
- How to Approach: Find licensed psychologists and mental health professionals in Paris for individual and couples counseling.

Fédération Nationale Solidarité Femmes (FNSF)

- Website: www.solidaritefemmes.org
- How to Approach: While focused on women, they provide resources and support for family members affected by domestic violence.

Denmark:

Manderådgivninge

- Website: www.manderaadgivningen.dk
- How to Approach: Seek support and counseling services tailored for men.

Mindhelper

- Website: www.mindhelper.dk
- How to Approach: Access mental health resources and online support for youth and adults.

Dansk Stalking Center

- Website: www.danskstalkingcenter.dk
- How to Approach: Find support for victims of stalking, including men.

Germany:

Männerhilfetelefon

- Website: www.maennerhilfetelefon.de
- Phone: 0800 1239900
- How to Approach: Call the helpline for support in cases of domestic abuse and emotional distress.

Pro Familia

- Website: www.profamilia.de
- How to Approach: Access family and relationship counseling services.

Deutsche Depressionshilfe

- Website: www.deutsche-depressionshilfe.de
- How to Approach: Find resources and support for dealing with depression.

Spain:

Asociación de Hombres por la Igualdad de Género (AHIGE)

- Website: www.ahige.org
- How to Approach: Explore resources and support groups for men.

Fundación ANAR

- Website: www.anar.org
- Phone: 900 20 20 10
- How to Approach: Call the helpline for support in cases of domestic violence.

Psicólogos Madrid

- Website: www.psicologosmadrid.org
- How to Approach: Find licensed psychologists and mental health professionals in Madrid.

Mexico:

Linea Nacional Contra la Violencia Doméstica

- Website: www.contralaviolenciadomestica.org.mx
- Phone: 800-911-25-66
- How to Approach: Call the helpline for support and resources related to domestic violence.

Red de Apoyo

- Website: www.reddeapoyo.org.mx
- How to Approach: Explore support services and counseling options for individuals facing emotional and relational challenges.

Psicólogos México

- Website: www.psicologosmexico.com
- How to Approach: Use the directory to find mental health professionals and book counseling sessions.

How to Approach Support Services

Identify Your Needs: Determine the type of support you need, whether emotional, legal, or financial.

- Research Options: Use the provided websites and contact information to explore the services available in your area.
- Make Contact: Contact support services via phone, email, or online chat to initiate contact. Be clear about your situation and what kind of help you're seeking.

- Follow-Up: If you don't receive a response or the service isn't a good fit, don't hesitate to contact another organization.
- Stay Persistent: Finding the proper support can take time and persistence. Keep seeking help until you find the resources that meet your needs.

Suicide Prevention: Reaching Out for Help

In times of crisis, it is crucial to seek support immediately. The following list provides contact information for suicide prevention centers and helplines worldwide. These resources offer confidential, 24/7 assistance to help you navigate challenging times and find hope. Remember, reaching out for help is a sign of strength and a vital step towards healing.

Contact Information for Support Groups and Counseling Services by Country

USA:

National Suicide Prevention Lifeline

- Website: www.suicidepreventionlifeline.org
- Phone: 1-800-273-TALK (8255)
- How to Approach: Call the helpline for confidential support, available 24/7. They also offer chat services on their website.

Crisis Text Line

- Website: www.crisistextline.org
- Text: Text HOME to 741741
- How to Approach: Text for immediate support from a trained crisis counselor.

UK:

Samaritans

- Website: www.samaritans.org
- Phone: 116 123
- How to Approach: Call or email for confidential support, available 24/7.

Papyrus UK (Prevention of Young Suicide)

- Website: www.papyrus-uk.org
- Phone: HOPELINEUK 0800 068 4141
- How to Approach: Call, text, or email for support. Available for young people up to age 35.

Australia:

Lifeline Australia

- Website: www.lifeline.org.au
- Phone: 13 11 14

- How to Approach: Call for 24/7 crisis support and suicide prevention services.

Beyond Blue

- Website: www.beyondblue.org.au
- Phone: 1300 22 4636
- How to Approach: Call or chat online with a trained mental health professional.

Canada:

Crisis Services Canada

- Website: www.crisisservicescanada.ca
- Phone: 1-833-456-4566
- Text: 45645
- How to Approach: Call or text for 24/7 crisis support.

Kids Help Phone (for youth)

- Website: www.kidshelpphone.ca
- Phone: 1-800-668-6868
- How to Approach: Call or text for confidential support available 24/7.

Italy:

Telefono Amico Italia

- Website: www.telefonoamico.it
- Phone: 199 284 284
- How to Approach: Call for emotional support and crisis intervention.

Samaritans Onlus

- Website: www.samaritansonlus.org
- Phone: 06 77208977
- How to Approach: Call for confidential support and help.

New Zealand:

Lifeline New Zealand

- Website: www.lifeline.org.nz
- Phone: 0800 543 354
- How to Approach: Call for 24/7 crisis support and suicide prevention services.

Youthline

- Website: www.youthline.co.nz
- Phone: 0800 376 633
- How to Approach: Call, text, or email for youth-focused support services.

India:

Snehi – Suicide Prevention Helpline

- Phone: 91-22-27721377
- How to Approach: Call for confidential support and crisis intervention.

AASRA

- Website: www.aasra.info
- Phone: 91-22-27546669
- How to Approach: Call for 24/7 suicide prevention and crisis support.

Japan:

Tokyo Mental Health

- Website: www.tokyomentalhealth.com
- How to Approach: Book online appointments for counseling and therapy services.

TELL Japan

- Website: www.telljp.com
- Phone: 03-5774-0992
- How to Approach: Call the lifeline for confidential support and counseling, available 24/7.

France:

SOS Suicide

- Website: www.sos-suicide.org
- Phone: 01 45 39 40 00
- How to Approach: Call for immediate support and crisis intervention.

SOS Suicide Jeunes (for youth)

- Website: www.sos-suicide.org
- Phone: 01 45 39 40 00
- How to Approach: Call for youth-specific suicide prevention and support.

Denmark:

Livslinien

- Website: www.livslinien.dk
- Phone: 70 201 201
- How to Approach: Call for crisis support and suicide prevention, available 24/7.

Headspace Denmark

- Website: www.headspace.dk
- How to Approach: Access mental health support services and counseling for young people.

Germany:

Telefonseelsorge Deutschland

- Website: www.telefonseelsorge.de
- Phone: 0800 111 0 111 / 0800 111 0 222
- How to Approach: Call for confidential support and counseling, available 24/7.

Deutsche Depressionshilfe

- Website: www.deutsche-depressionshilfe.de
- How to Approach: Find resources and support for dealing with depression and suicidal thoughts.

Spain:

Teléfono de la Esperanza

- Website: www.telefonodelaesperanza.org
- Phone: 717 003 717
- How to Approach: Call for emotional support and crisis intervention, available 24/7.

ANAR Foundation (for youth)

- Website: www.anar.org
- Phone: 900 20 20 10
- How to Approach: Call the helpline for youth-specific support and counseling.

Mexico:

Línea Nacional Contra el Suicidio

- Phone: 800 273 8255
- How to Approach: Call for immediate crisis support and suicide prevention services.

SAPTEL

- Website: www.saptel.org.mx
- Phone: 55 5259 8121
- How to Approach: Call for emotional support and crisis intervention, available 24/7.

How to Approach Support Services

Recognize the Need for Help:

- Seeking help is a sign of strength and a step toward healing.
- Use provided phone numbers or websites for immediate support. Many services offer 24-hour assistance.
- Be Open and Honest: When contacting a helpline or support service, express your feelings and situation. Trained professionals are ready to assist you without judgment.
- Follow Recommendations. Listen to the support professionals' advice and recommendations. They can provide resources and strategies to help you get through your crisis.
- Seek Ongoing Support: After initial contact, consider seeking counseling, support groups, or therapy to continue

healing.

Reaching out is a brave step toward reclaiming your well-being and restoring hope.

Chapter 13: Why is it so hard for men to find people to talk to?

Many men find it difficult, if not impossible, to find someone with whom to discuss their deepest concerns and emotions. This chapter highlights the various reasons men often struggle to open up and seek help and offers strategies for overcoming these obstacles.

The Social Stigma of Male Vulnerability

- One of the most pervasive barriers to men seeking help is society's attachment to male vulnerability. From a young age, many men are taught that expressing emotions and discussing personal issues is a sign of weakness.
- Judgment and Perception: Men are often judged harshly for discussing sensitive or emotional topics. Men may fear being perceived as weak or incapable, which prevents them from speaking up.
- Cultural Expectations: Men's traditional gender roles emphasize stoicism and emotional restraint, perpetuating the belief that they should handle problems independently.

The Fear of Burdening Others

Another significant barrier is the fear of burdening friends or family members with their problems. Men may be concerned that sharing their struggles will cause undue stress in their relationships or that their concerns will be dismissed.

- Men may suppress their struggles due to a sense of responsibility to protect those they care about.
- Men often minimize their problems, believing they can handle them without relying on others.

The Challenge of Finding Relatable Support

Many men struggle to find people who can truly understand their problems. This can be especially difficult when dealing with specific or unique issues that must be better understood or recognized.

- Men may feel isolated in their experiences, believing others do not understand or empathize.
- Certain issues, such as emotional abuse in relationships, may necessitate specialized support that is not widely available or recognized.

The Demands of Work and Family Life

Balancing work and family responsibilities gives men little time to seek out and engage in supportive conversations. The demands of daily life can make it challenging to prioritize emotional well-being.

- Men face time constraints due to busy schedules and responsibilities, making it difficult to maintain supportive relationships.
- Men may prioritize their family and work over their well-being, leaving less time for self-care and support.
- Avoidance of Uncomfortable Conversations. Another barrier is the discomfort of talking about personal and emotional issues. Many people, including men, avoid conversations about uncomfortable or painful topics. Social norms often prioritize light, superficial topics over deeper, emotional conversations, making it difficult to discuss personal issues.
- Men may avoid uncomfortable conversations for fear of rejection or negative judgment.

The Difficulty in Finding Support Networks

Even when men are willing to seek support, finding appropriate and accessing resources and networks can be difficult. Many men are unsure where to turn or how to find others dealing with similar issues.

- Men may not be aware of available support groups, organizations, or online communities that meet their needs.
- Certain support networks may be inaccessible due to location, cost, or other factors.

The Struggle to Start Meaningful Conversations

Starting meaningful conversations about personal struggles can be extremely difficult for men. Initiating such discussions is often fraught with inexperience and lack of confidence.

- Men may struggle to express their emotions and concerns effectively, leading to hesitation in starting conversations.
- Men used to maintaining a solid and composed exterior may struggle to open up due to their fear of vulnerability.

Overcoming the Barriers

Despite these challenges, men can get the help they need. Here are some strategies for overcoming these barriers:

- Actively challenge societal norms related to male vulnerability. Encourage open conversations about emotions and mental health with friends and family.
- Seek professional help: A therapist or counselor can offer a safe and confidential space to discuss personal issues.
- Join Support Groups: Find local or online groups that address specific issues. These groups foster a sense of community and understanding.
- Prioritize Self-Care: Focus on your emotional well-being. This could entail setting aside time each week to connect with supportive individuals.
- Practice communication skills by expressing your emotions and concerns. Begin with small, trusted circles and gradually expand.
- Use online resources and forums to connect with others experiencing similar challenges. Reddit, specialized forums, and mental health websites can be valuable resources.

You know, finding people to talk to about personal issues is difficult but possible. You can seek the help you need and remember that asking for help is a sign of strength, and developing a network of supportive relationships is critical for emotional health.

Chapter 14: Planning for Change

lanning for change can be both liberating and intimidating when dealing with a problematic marriage. It entails making essential decisions about your future, assessing the viability of remaining in the marriage, and taking steps to protect yourself and your interests. This chapter will walk you through evaluating your situation, developing a plan for personal and relational change, understanding legal and financial implications, and ensuring your safety during this transitional period.

Before making significant changes, consider whether staying in the marriage is viable and beneficial to your well-being. Consider the following factors:

Developing a Plan for Personal and Relational Change

After you've assessed your situation, you should create a concrete plan for personal and relational change. This plan should include specific steps to improve your well-being and relationship dynamics.

- Set clear goals for yourself and your relationship. Goals should be specific, measurable, achievable, relevant, and time-bound (SMART).

- Seek professional help, such as individual or couples therapy, to address underlying issues and implement positive change strategies. A therapist can offer guidance and support throughout the process.
- Improve communication skills by expressing needs, actively listening, and effectively resolving conflicts. Open and honest communication is essential for relational change.
- Focus on Self-Care: Prioritize your physical, mental, and emotional health. Engage in activities that promote self-care, such as exercise, hobbies, and mindfulness practices.
- Evaluate Progress: Regularly assess your goals' progress and the relationship's overall health. Be prepared to make adjustments as needed.

Legal and Financial Considerations in the Event of Separation or Divorce

If remaining in the marriage is not an option, understanding separation or divorce's legal and financial implications is critical. Proper planning protects your rights and interests at this difficult time.

- Consult a lawyer. Seek legal advice to understand your rights and obligations better. A lawyer can help you navigate the process and make informed decisions.
- Assess your financial situation. List all your assets, debts, income, and expenses to understand your finances.
- Create a budget for your post-separation or divorce finan-

cial situation—account for living expenses, legal fees, and any potential changes in income.

- Property and Asset Division: Determine how property and assets will be distributed. This could include the family home, savings, investments, and personal belongings.
- If you have children, resolve child support and custody issues. Ensure that the children's best interests are prioritized.
- Documentation: Maintain detailed records of all financial transactions, communications, and legal documents. Proper documentation is necessary to protect your interests.

Steps to Protect Yourself and Your Interests

Protecting yourself and your interests during this period entails taking proactive steps to ensure your safety, security, and well-being.

- Build a support network of friends, family, and professionals who can offer emotional and practical support.
- Secure essential documents, including identification, financial records, legal papers, and personal items. Store copies in a secure location.
- Develop a safety plan in case of abuse or unsafe situations. This could include finding a safe place to stay, making emergency contacts, and seeking legal assistance.
- Establish financial independence by opening separate bank and credit card accounts.
- Monitor Your Credit: Regularly check your credit report to ensure no unauthorized transactions or accounts are opened in your name.

- Stay Informed: Keep yourself informed about your legal rights and options. Knowledge is a powerful tool for protecting your interests.

Chapter 15: Moving Forward

Leaving a difficult marriage is essential to reclaiming your life and well-being. While complex, the journey of healing and recovery provides an opportunity to rebuild self-esteem, rediscover personal passions, and prepare for healthier future relationships. This chapter delves into the steps for healing and recovery after leaving a difficult marriage, including rebuilding self-esteem, tips for entering new relationships with a healthy mindset, and maintaining long-term emotional and mental well-being.

Healing and Recovery After Leaving a Difficult Marriage

The end of a difficult marriage can bring up a wide range of emotions, from relief and freedom to grief and uncertainty. Healing and recovery are essential for navigating these emotions and rebuilding your life.

- Recognize the end of your marriage and allow yourself to grieve the loss. It is natural to experience sadness, anger, and confusion. Allow yourself to experience these emotions without judgment.

- Seek support from friends, family, and professionals who can offer emotional and practical assistance. Join support groups to share your experiences and connect with others who understand your situation.
- Individual therapy can help you explore feelings, gain insights, and develop coping strategies. A therapist can help you navigate the healing process and build resilience.
- Practice self-compassion and acknowledge that healing takes time. Avoid blaming yourself or engaging in negative self-talk. Treat yourself with the compassion you would show a friend in a similar situation.
- Prioritize living in the moment and planning for the future over reflecting on the past. Engage in activities that give you joy and fulfillment.

Rebuilding Self-Esteem and Rediscovering Personal Passions

Rebuilding self-esteem and rediscovering personal passions are critical steps toward reclaiming your identity and living a fulfilling life after a difficult marriage.

- Recognize and celebrate your achievements, no matter how small. Recognizing your progress boosts your self-esteem and motivates you to keep going.
- Set personal goals. Identify goals that are consistent with your values and interests. Setting and achieving goals, whether related to your career, a hobby, or personal development, gives you a sense of purpose and accomplishment.
- Rediscover hobbies that bring joy and fulfillment. Engaging in creative or physical activities can be therapeutic and allow you to reconnect with your interests.

- Focus on your unique strengths and qualities to develop a positive self-image. Surround yourself with positive influences and affirmations that promote a healthy self-image.
- Volunteering and giving back can give you a sense of purpose and connect you with your community. Helping others can boost your self-esteem and provide a sense of purpose.

Tips for Entering New Relationships with a Healthy Mindset

Entering new relationships after leaving a difficult marriage necessitates a positive mindset and a commitment to your well-being and boundaries.

- Give yourself time to heal and rebuild before starting a new relationship. Rushing into a new relationship without addressing past wounds can result in recurring patterns and unresolved issues.
- Reflect on Past Experiences: Learn from your previous marriage and identify patterns to avoid. Use these insights to help you approach new relationships.
- Establish clear boundaries and communicate them early in the relationship. Healthy boundaries are necessary for mutual respect and emotional safety.
- Encourage open, honest communication with your new partner. Please openly share your thoughts, feelings, and needs with your partner and encourage them to do the same.
- Prioritize self-care and well-being. A healthy relationship should enhance your life, not take away from it.

Maintaining Long-Term Emotional and Mental Well-Being

Long-term emotional and mental well-being necessitates continuous self-care, self-awareness, and proactive strategies for maintaining balance and resilience.

- Establish a self-care routine: Create a self-care routine incorporating physical, emotional, and mental health practices. Regular exercise, mindfulness, and relaxation techniques can help you maintain balance and resilience.
- Stay connected with friends, family, and support networks. Social connections offer emotional support and alleviate feelings of isolation.
- Encourage personal growth through education, hobbies, and new experiences. Lifelong learning and development contribute to a fulfilling and meaningful existence.
- Monitor your mental health: Regularly check in with yourself and monitor your mental health. If you are experiencing stress, anxiety, or depression, seek professional help.
- Practice Gratitude: Cultivate an attitude of gratitude by regularly reflecting on the positive aspects of your life. Gratitude can enhance your overall sense of well-being and happiness.

Closing Chapter: Strength, Resilience, and New Beginnings

As we end our journey together, it's time to reflect on the key lessons and strategies covered in this book. The path to healing and growth amid a problematic marriage takes work. Still, it reveals your inner strength and resilience. Let's review the key insights, encourage continued growth and healing, and offer some final thoughts on resilience and self-discovery. This conclusion is an inspirational message to enable you to overcome obstacles and embrace a brighter future.

Encouragement to Continue Seeking Growth and Healing

Healing and growth are ongoing processes that necessitate sustained effort and dedication. As you progress, remember to stay committed to your healing journey. Every step forward, no matter how small, represents progress.

- Embrace Change: Be open to new experiences. Stepping outside of your comfort zone is often beneficial for personal growth.
- Continue seeking support from friends, family, and profes-

sionals. You do not have to face this journey alone.

- Practice self-compassion and acknowledge that healing takes time. Celebrate your accomplishments and forgive yourself for any setbacks.

Final Thoughts on the Journey of Resilience and Self-Discovery

The journey through a difficult marriage and beyond is a profound lesson in resilience and self-discovery. It demonstrates your ability to persevere, adapt, and grow despite adversity. Embracing resilience entails recognizing your strength and using it as a foundation for a brighter future.

- Resilience involves facing challenges with courage and emerging stronger rather than avoiding them altogether.
- Self-discovery: Reflect on your identity, values, and goals during this journey. Accept the person you're becoming.

Inspirational Message to Empower Readers to Overcome Their Challenges

As you close this book, remember you are not alone in your struggle. Your pain is confirmed, your experiences are valid, and your journey to healing and growth demonstrates your strength.

You are capable of overcoming life's challenges. You can lead a fulfilling and joyful life by embracing resilience, setting boundaries, seeking support, and committing to personal growth. Your past does not define you; your current actions and choices shape your future.

Believe in yourself, trust your abilities, and live a life that values your worth and well-being. You are capable of great things, and the road ahead is full of opportunities for development and happiness.

Authors Note: The Journey Behind Silent Sufferings of Men

I grew up hearing stories about silent suffering. Growing up, I witnessed the pain and struggles of men in my immediate circle, including friends, family members, and neighbors, each with their own story of heartache and perseverance. These were men who exuded strength and resilience on the outside. Still, behind closed doors, they were silently suffering from emotional and psychological distress.

The inspiration for Silent Sufferings of Men stems from intensely personal observations and experiences in the lives of men around me—men who suffered silently beneath the veneer of strength that society expects them to maintain. From a young age, I became aware of the emotional and psychological struggles that men face, often within the confines of difficult marriages.

During a recent road trip with some close friends, we decided to visit an old friend, Mr. Felix, whom we hadn't seen or spoken to in over ten years. Felix had once been the glue that held our community together—kind, dependable, and always willing to lend a hand. We admired, respected, and thought about him frequently. But no one knew what had happened to him in all these years.

When we arrived at his door, the man who greeted us was not the Felix we knew. The robust and warm figure was gone, replaced by someone who appeared much older than his age, worn down by life. We quickly realized why. Behind his calm and gentle demeanor lay a heartbreaking story of silent suffering. His marriage had become a prison, where his wife used emotional abuse with precision.

She used societal norms, which expect men to be stoic and strong, to her advantage. She completely controlled Felix's life, including his finances, interactions, and emotions. Worse, she manipulated their teenage son, turning him against his father. They insulted and humiliated Felix in front of his family and friends. The verbal abuse escalated into physical confrontations, with Felix receiving beatings and constant harassment. His dignity was eroded with each insult and blow.

This emotional warfare had its toll. Felix sank into a deep depression, feeling wholly cut off from the people he loved. He was unable to communicate freely with his friends or pay visits to his aging mother. The weight of the abuse and stress eventually caused a heart attack, leaving him partially paralyzed. He lost his high-paying job and the life he had worked hard to build.

Seeing Felix after so many years was a heartbreaking experience. He had aged beyond his years, and his spirit had been broken. His story was one of pain and loneliness—a man trapped in a situation he couldn't get out of, too afraid to speak up, and too ashamed to seek help. Society had failed him, forcing him into a corner where he felt his pain was invalid and he had no right to express his distress.

This story, along with countless others I've heard, has made me realize the gravity of the situation. Men, like women, are humans with emotional vulnerabilities. However, the world frequently expects them to be stoic, to suffer in silence, and to "handle it." This expectation prevents them from expressing their pain and seeking assistance.

Writing this book became more than a mission; it was a respon-sibility to give voice to the many men like Felix who have been marginalized, misunderstood, and left to suffer in silence. It evolved into an attempt to remove the stigma associated with male vulnerability and to provide strategies for men to navigate the complexities of difficult marriages. I wanted to provide a lifeline, a sense of validation, and a road map for healing and empowerment.

These experiences fueled a fire within me, a desire to break the silence and shed light on the hidden struggles of men in difficult marriages. I felt compelled to give those who had been silenced a voice, to acknowledge their pain, and to offer a path to healing and empowerment.

This book will provide practical strategies, advice, and a sense of validation and understanding. I want every man who reads these pages to understand that his pain is real, his struggles are legitimate, and he is not alone. There is hope, solutions, and a way to lead a more fulfilling life.

Thank you for reading Silent Sufferings of Men, Your feedback is precious and helps me improve future editions. Please leave a review on the platform where you purchased the book. Your honest thoughts can guide other readers and further discussions around this important topic.

If you have any questions or would like to reach out to me directly, feel free to contact me at praveekk@yahoo.com

I appreciate your support!

Yours truly,

Praveen Kottepaka

Appendix: Resources and Further Reading

As you continue your healing and growth journey, having access to additional resources can be a great source of support and guidance. This appendix contains a list of recommended books, articles, websites, and contact information for support groups and counseling services. It also includes practical exercises and worksheets for self-reflection and growth.

A list of recommended books, articles, and websites

Books:

- John M. Gottman and Nan Silver's "The Seven Principles for Making Marriage Work" is a research-based guide to building and maintaining a healthy marriage.
- Gary Chapman's "The 5 Love Languages: The Secret to Love that Lasts" explores the various ways people express and receive love and provides insights to improve relationships.
- Hold Me Tight: Seven Conversations for a Lifetime of Love by Dr. Sue Johnson
- Introduces Emotionally Focused Therapy (EFT) and offers

practical strategies for enhancing emotional connection in relationships.
- Mating in Captivity: Unlocking Erotic Intelligence by Esther Perel
- Examines the challenges of maintaining desire and intimacy in long-term relationships.
- Too Good to Leave, Too Bad to Stay: A Step-by-Step Guide to Help You Decide Whether to Stay In or Get Out of Your Relationship by Mira Kirshenbaum
- Provides a framework for evaluating whether to remain in or leave a troubled relationship.
- His Needs, Her Needs: Building an Affair-Proof Marriage by Willard F. Harley Jr.
- Identifies the top emotional needs of men and women and offers strategies for meeting those needs.

Articles:

- The Impact of Emotional Abuse in Marriage" by Psychology Today, An article exploring the effects of emotional abuse on mental health and well-being.
- How to Recognize and Handle Gaslighting in Relationships by Very well Mind, Provides information on identifying gas lighting and strategies for dealing with it.
- Building Emotional Resilience: Tips and Strategies" by Harvard Health Publishing. Offers practical advice for developing emotional resilience.

Practical exercises and worksheets for self-reflection and growth

Self-Reflection Exercises:

1. Journaling prompts:
   Respond to prompts to reflect on your experiences and emotions. Examples include:

   - What are my core values, and how do they impact my decisions?
   - What lessons have I learned from my marriage?
   - Identify your strengths and use them to overcome challenges.

2. Gratitude journal:

Every day, write down three things for which you are grateful. This practice can help you focus on the positive aspects of your life.

Worksheets:

   - Worksheet for Setting Boundaries: - Identify areas for setting boundaries and outline actions to establish and maintain them.
   - Goal Setting Worksheet: - Use the SMART criteria to define short- and long-term goals (Specific, Measurable, Attainable, Relevant, Time-bound).
   - Use the Emotional Awareness Worksheet to track your emotions throughout the day, including triggers and responses. This can help you better understand and control your emotional reactions.

Mindfulness Practices:

- Practice mindful breathing by focusing on your breath for a few minutes daily. Inhale deeply and exhale slowly, focusing on the sensation of the breath entering and leaving your body.
- Practice Body Scan Meditation to relax and connect with your body. Begin at your toes and gradually work your way up to your head, noticing and releasing any tension you may feel.

Resources:

- American Psychological Association (APA) – Infidelity and Marital Conflict.
- Journal of Marriage and Family – Factors Influencing Marital Infidelity.
- Psychology Today – The Dynamics of Infidelity.
- Wikipedia
- https://pmc.ncbi.nlm.nih.gov/articles/PMC8209536/

Also by Praveen Kottepaka

THE JOB JAIL BREAK : 10 Strategies to Kick Start Your Own Business and to Kick Off Your 9-to-5 Grind.

The Power of This Book: The Book That Will Reshape Your Life's Narrative.

Unlock Your Freedom with "The JOB JAIL BREAK"

Tired of the 9-to-5 grind? Ready to break free from the daily routine and live on your own terms?

☆ My book, **"The JOB JAIL BREAK,"** is here to help you kickstart your journey to personal and financial freedom!

✦ In this empowering guide, you will discover:

🔑 Proven strategies to escape the traditional job cycle

💡 Innovative ideas to launch and grow your own business

📈 Inspiring success stories of entrepreneurs who took the leap

⚡ Practical tips for achieving autonomy and empowerment

Welcome to the "The Job Jail Break," and welcome to the first day of the rest of your life....

THE JOB JAIL BREAK 10 Strategies to Kick Start Your Own Business and to Kick Off Your 9-to-5 Grind

https://a.co/d/bcDjpP1